Beating the bullies

HOW DID BEN HELP HIMSELF?

JCP

First published by
Jane Curry Publishing 2012
[Wentworth Concepts Pty Ltd]
PO Box 780 Edgecliff NSW 2027 Australia
www.janecurrypublishing.com.au

National Library of Australia Cataloguing-in-Publication entry

Author: Blunt, Lucy.
Title: Beating the bullies : terrific tips to empower your
            kids / Lucy Blunt ; illustrations by Chloe Osborn.

ISBN: 9780987227539 (pbk.)

Subjects: Bullying in schools--Juvenile literature.
            Bullying--Prevention--Juvenile literature.
            Bullying--Psychological aspects.

Other Authors/Contributors: Osborn, Chloe.

Dewey Number: 371.58

Cover and internal illustrations: Chloe Osborn
Cover and internal design: Wendy Rapee
Production: Karen Young
Printed in China by 1010 Printing

Contents

Dedication

For Papa/Peter and Eloise — whom we love always

For all of our spectacular extended family — for their love, support, care and laughter

For the dream team: Caroline, Carolyn, Chris, Kellie, Penny and Theresa — for everything

For our fabulous friends — who also doubled as proofreaders and commentators...

For Wendy and Jane — who yet again made it a fabulous book.

And finally, for all of those wonderful children and families with whom I have had the honour to work alongside during their struggles in dealing with the pain of bullying...

Lucy and Chloe

Chapter one
"My friend" has a problem

My friend is being **bullied**. He is my age, my height **and he looks an awful lot like me.** I told my mum a while ago that my friend

was being bullied. I said two children in his class had **hidden his lunch** at the bottom of the lost property basket.

She was doing the washing up and I don't think she was really **listening** properly. She said, "*Oh, that wasn't very kind was it?*" And then she kept on doing the washing up. I didn't know what to do then. I didn't know how to tell her **it was actually ME who was being bullied.**

The next night Dad was reading the paper when I went to talk to him. I told him that **my friend** was being ***bullied***. Dad asked how he was being bullied.

I said, "They **PUSHED** him on the bus and **KICKED** his school bag off and then they called him

names. It's making him feel lousy and he doesn't want to go to school anymore."

I couldn't bear to tell Dad it was **really me**, his son Ben who was being **bullied**. After all, I'm tall and normal looking with brown hair and blue eyes. I like sport, playing computer games, playing chess with my dad or riding my bike or my scooter if we go somewhere. I have a regular family, just like any other kid.

Dad went back to reading the paper and said, "Well, he's just going to

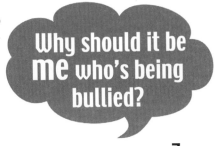
Why should it be **me** who's being bullied?

have to toughen up isn't he. He's just going to have to grow a thicker skin."

I didn't know what he meant by that. How do you toughen up? **HOW DO you grow thick skin?**

Chapter two
Mum and Dad figure it out

At dinner the next night, I could tell that Mum and Dad had been talking. They looked like they were working  themselves up to say something. Mum finally said, "Ben, which one of your friends is being bullied?"

I didn't know what to say. **I felt *really* embarrassed.** I looked up in the air and said, **"Oh, no one YOU know.**  It's just someone I know from... around." Mum and Dad looked at each other and said, "Ben, if you are being bullied, we can help you. We are a family, and we look after each other, **but you need to tell us what has been happening."**

Hmmm... I was **STUCK**. I didn't know what to do. I really liked the idea that my family might help me, but on the other hand, it sure was embarrassing. **I felt like I shouldn't need help.** I felt as though if I needed help, then I was **a loser**. I also didn't know what to say. My parents both have lots of friends and I feel like I don't have any. How do you say, "I'm so **lonely** at school. Everyone else has a friend or a group of friends, and I don't. Even when I think I've made friends, they just start being nasty to me." I didn't know how to tell them about the boys from school who say really *horrible things*, **SHOVE ME** on the school bus and then try to **CHASE ME** home. I didn't know how to tell them how

scared and **SAD** it makes me feel or about how I lie awake at night with a **sore tummy** wishing I could go to a different school.

So I looked at my parents and they looked at me. "Nah, everything's fine," I said.

My little sister Harriet giggled. She sang out,

"Ben's got no friends. Ben's got no friends.

He walks around the playground at lunchtime by himself, because everybody hates him!!"

Chapter three
Telling (OOH, SO embarrassing)

Well, boy oh boy, you should have seen the **firecrackers** go off in our house!!

Mum got **REALLY** cross with Harriet and put her in her room (I quite liked that bit). She then said we should sit down and talk about what had been happening at school **(this bit I didn't like so much)**. It kind of felt *nice and warm* to talk to Mum, like being tucked up in bed at night, but it was also a bit like sitting outside the Principal's office waiting for him to come out. Dad came too and sat with his arm around me while Mum rubbed my leg. They asked me about what had been happening. I couldn't talk much, **but I cried a lot.**

Finally I told them about Sam and Damien and the other boys and how **MEAN** they were being at school. Mum said we needed an **ACTION PLAN** (she loves a plan). She said she was going to talk to the Principal at my school and also ring a psychologist friend of hers — to help me with some tips

16

and ideas. I was so **embarrassed** and SCARED when Mum said she was going to talk to the school. I begged her not to! I said if the other kids found out I had told on them, it was just going to make it **WORSE**. Mum said bullying was a school problem and we needed the school's help to sort it out. She said it was a teacher's job to make sure all the children are safe at school and to make sure everyone is playing well together. She said that until the **bullies** were exposed and told their behaviour was unacceptable, the bullying would keep happening.

I still felt really SCARED, but I kind of knew she was right.

Chapter four
Telling the school (yikes!!)

The next day I said I had a
sore tummy and I couldn't go
to school. Mum said I was being

ridiculous
and that
everything
would be
all right.
I started
crying. I was
so **woRRieD**

about going to school and worried
about what everyone would say when

they got into trouble. I turned over and said my tummy hurt even more. Mum said *a good dose of pancakes always helped a scared tummy* — but only when I was dressed for school. I thought pancakes might help too. They were yummy, and they did help — for a bit.

Mum and Dad took me to school and they went to see the Principal, Mr Johnson, while I went to class. Sam *tripped* me up just as I was about to sit down. I looked around, but the teacher was writing on the board and everyone else pretended nothing had happened — except for Mandy up the back — who giggled. I felt **alone** and small.

Chapter five
The bullies find out

At break time, I played by myself on the play equipment. At lunchtime I read a new book... up until the other kids came and told me I was

a "**Reading Freak**". It felt **really bad** to have the one thing I really enjoyed picked on.

After lunch, Sam and Damien were asked to go to Mr Johnson's office. When they came back, they didn't look at me when they sat down. Sam looked **FUR!OUS**. Damien looked like he had been **crying**. Even though they hadn't looked at me, I just knew the meeting had been about the bullying. I felt **VERY** SCARED. I wondered what would happen after school.

Chapter six
Getting some help

After school, Dad came to the
classroom to pick me up. He
NEVER does that. He's usually at
work. He said to me, "Mum has
an appointment for all of us with
her friend Teresa, the psychologist.

Quickly, let's get Harriet; we've got to get there soon." We raced to find Harriet and got in the car. **It felt great** not having to get on the bus with Damien and Sam. I wished I could do that every day.

Teresa was fantastic!! She was really nice and very funny. She told me she was a Clinical Psychologist and she worked with children. She told me an amazing thing. **LOTS OF KIDS GET BULLIED** — and not just boys, but girls too! I asked her how girls get bullied — because I never see it at school. She told me that there are two types of bullying.

Overt bullying is when someone says something mean out loud, or hits you, or does something obviously **NASTY**. **Covert bullying** though is when they do something **SNEAKY**, which you find out later — or when they keep leaving you out of games and either won't let you play, or make you be the stupid or the baby one in the game — **or the dog**.

I thought of my friend Ruby, and how the girls **hadn't let her** pl**ay** with them last year, or always made her be the one who **held** the jump rope when they were skipping and never let her have a turn. I thought about how upset she had been then. **I hadn't really understood**, but I had invited her to play with me if she was on her own or looked sad.

Chapter seven
I tell Teresa

Teresa asked me about what had been happening at school. It felt **weird** to talk about it; but I told her about the boys **H!D!NG** my lunch so I couldn't find it, about them **K!CK!NG** my school bag off the

bus, **TR!PPING** me up in class and sometimes **CHAS!NG** me.
I also told her how they said that everything I liked doing (like playing

chess or riding my scooter) was stupid and babyish

and that I wasn't cool enough to play with them. I said that when we were in class, they would tread on my things when they walked past, and in sport they wouldn't choose me to be on their team.

Teresa said this must have felt **REALLY bad** and asked me how long the bullying had been going on. I told her it had been happening for most of this year. She asked if I had ever tried playing with any other children. I said I'd tried — but I **REALLY liked** playing with Damien and Sam and Andy, because they played interesting games. The problem was, just as it was becoming **fun**, someone would push or shove me, or trip me up, or do something to **HURT MY FEELINGS**. Then they would all laugh at me and go off on their own. Teresa said "Hmmm... You think they play interesting games? Well

I don't think so! If those kids aren't being nice, then their games aren't interesting — they're bad for your health!"

I laughed, but said that while the other kids I had tried to play with were nice, they didn't like the same things I did and **I felt like I didn't fit in with their group**. Teresa said that **LOTS** of kids feel like this, and sometimes it is only when new people come to the school, or you move on to another school, that you find someone who is more like you. She said you don't really know if you will fit in with another group of kids until you

actually play with them a few times. She said maybe I was just guessing they weren't as much fun as Damien, Sam and Andy, when they might actually be even more fun to play with. And they might be nicer!!

Then Teresa asked a strange thing. She said, "Do you see how you are sitting right now? Do you always sit like that? With your head down and not looking at anyone when you're talking?" I said I didn't know. She said there were lots of things we would work on together♡ which would help sort out the bullying problem, and how I looked when I sat

34

or stood was just one of them.

Teresa said we needed an **ACTION PLAN** (another one!). This would be a list of things I could try out at school. She said some things would work when I tried them and some wouldn't. She said **EVERYONE IS DIFFERENT**, and some things work better for some children than others. She told me it would take a few weeks of me coming to see her to work out which ones were the right ones for me; so we needed to get started straight away!

I felt a bit **excited**. Maybe something could help after all?

Chapter eight
Teresa's terrific tips

So we got started on Teresa's whiteboard. This was our **ACTION PLAN.**

ACTION PLAN

1. Expose the bully (this has to be done by the Principal and the School Counsellor).

2. Learn the *Tough Talking Game*.

3. Use your *Personal Force Shield*.

4. Learn to walk away – don't keep the fight going.

5. Stay away from places in the playground where the bullying usually happens.

6. Try some new games and new people.

I was a bit confused about some of this, but Teresa explained each of the points on the list:

1. Expose The bully (to be done
by the Principal and the School
Counsellor) — Teresa said there are
bullies in every school, but some
schools don't have as much bullying
as others because the bullies have
been identified and told it is not
okay to be a bully. These schools
have a **Zero Tolerance** rule, which
means you are **NEVER** allowed to bully
someone else, and if you do, then
you get into trouble. First you get
into trouble from the teacher and
then the Principal calls your parents
in. Teresa said that schools like this
are happier because everyone knows

the **bullying is** unacceptable. She said the first step for us was for Mum and Dad to tell the school what had been happening, so the Principal and the School Counsellor could get involved. Then Sam and Damien and the other boys would know they were in trouble and would keep getting into trouble if they kept being bullies.

2. Learn The **Tough Talking Game** (and practise it with Teresa and my family):

The Tough Talking Game

Use your body:

■ **Head straight up and looking forward**

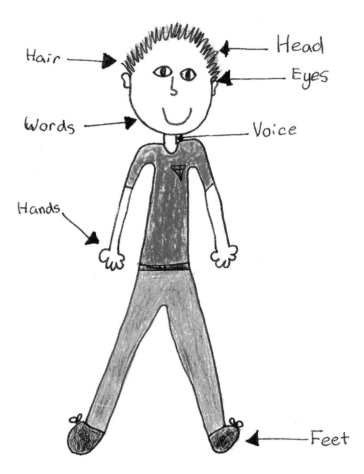

(like someone is pulling string up through your head like a puppet).

■ **Hair out of your face** (not falling across your eyes) so others can see you.

■ **Eyes straight ahead** (not looking up or down) and **DON'T MAKE EYE CONTACT** (Teresa says to look at the bullies' **EAR LOBES**, because this way it makes it seem as though you are looking at their eyes, when really you are imagining them with big fake rubber ears on and making yourself laugh inside!).

■ **Hands relaxed by your side** (not

rubbing them together nervously or crossing them in front of your chest).

■ **Feet firmly on the ground** (not changing from foot to foot) and no running away (being chased is not fun!). Don't give up your personal space by backing away.

■ **Make sure you take up a lot of physical room**; like a big strong superhero or wrestler (think about how much space a wrestler takes up when they walk — arms and shoulders out to the sides — not a quivering little mouse in a corner squeaking away).

■ Use your voice

▶ **Use a nice strong voice** (not a high, mousy one)

▶ **Use your words** — but don't turn it into a verbal fight. Say things that show you don't care, like "*Whatever*" or "*Big Deal*" or "*Well, that's only what you think*" or "*Tell someone who cares.*" Say these words, even if you do care, because then the bullies are not getting the reaction they wanted. But do not be rude — no point you getting into trouble too!!

3. Switch on your Personal Force Shield — Teresa said this is a secret force shield which gets activated whenever I do up my shoelaces! The best thing you can do if a bully is trying to stare you down is to break eye contact, take a deep breath and do something else. She said if you do something like tie up your shoelaces (even if they don't need doing), then you can activate a magic force field, which is like a shield that the bully's words hit and fly off again, so they don't hurt you. I thought this sounded COOL — like Star Wars!!

4. Learn to walk away — don't

keep the fight going — even if they are being unfair or rude. Teresa said that sometimes kids get picked on because they try and stick up for themselves or try and tell the other kids they're wrong and are being unfair. Walking away is sometimes the absolutely best option, and it is not the same as giving in. Some bullies don't care if they are being unfair or wrong, so arguing is a waste of time. She also said some bullies NEVER get it — so don't waste your breath.

5. Stay away from places in the playground where the bullying

usually happens — Teresa explained
that bullying often happens in certain
"spots" in the playground, because the
bullies know the places that teachers
don't go very often and which are
hard for them to supervise easily (like
behind our bike shed or the toilet
block). We drew a map of the school
and I showed her some of the areas
where the bullying usually takes place
— and I could see she was right!!

6. TRY SOME new GAMES and
new people — Teresa said this is
important! Give new things a try —
even if the kids seem a bit different to
you, or their games seem boring. Take

a new ball (a handball, a basketball) to school and start a new game with *different people*. You might feel a whole lot better, a whole lot faster. She also said to invite some different people home for a play. She said as long as afternoon tea was good, they would be happy to keep coming over!! I said maybe I could try a new sport and Teresa said sometimes joining a new team or group, like soccer or tennis or Scouts can help you make new friends: people who might like you and make you feel good about yourself. She said this was a good way to realise it was just a few mean kids giving you a rough time, rather than feeling as though **NOBODY** liked you. She said I should also spend time with people who make me feel *happy* — my cousins or other family friends — so I could remember **I am a terrific kid** (even if I don't really feel like it right now).

48

Chapter nine

Practising the tips

Then Teresa did something
weird!! She said we needed to start
ACTING (can you believe it?) First
of all, I had to tell her the kinds of
things I did which Sam would tease
me about and what he would usually

say. Then she pretended to be Sam and we acted out what would happen when he started bullying me. **This was really hard for me** because even though I knew it was Teresa, it still seemed really real and I felt sad and SCARED all over again.

BUT THEN... we changed roles and I had to be Sam and Teresa pretended to be me. This was fantastic!! It was fantastic because I saw what I looked like when I was being scared (**little** and frightened) and I got to try out how Sam feels when he is being tough (strong and powerful — but also really mean).

Then we did it again, but differently. This time Teresa was a whole new me. She was a TOUGH me. She was a me who stood my ground. She was

The new Magnificent ME!!!

a me who knew what to say, where to look and how to act. She was a Magnificent me!!! **i loved** her version of me!!! Teresa made me practise and practise until I got the hang of being a new, cool me. It took ages! It was fun; but I was still a bit scared. Would I be able to do it in front of Sam???

Chapter ten
Understanding the bully

At the end of the session, Teresa asked if I knew why some kids were bullies. I said I'd been too busy feeling scared and worried to think about *why* they might be so mean. It turns out there's a whole list of reasons why kids might be bullies:

Why bullies might be bullies

1. They might be **unhappy** or **lonely** and bullying makes them feel better about themselves (how weird is that?).

2. Something **bad** might be happening in their family (their parents might be getting a divorce or someone might be sick).

3. Their parents might be really strict and the only place the bully can **be in charge** is at school.

4. Their parents or other family members might be bullies too and that's the **only way** they know how to be.

5. They might be trying to **fit in** and get new friends and they think bullying is the only way they can do it.

6. They just **feel like it** (yeekkk!!).

Often bullies aren't really mean, they're just un happy. I thought about Sam and realised that he has two other big brothers who are pretty **MEAN TO HIM** (a bit like he is to me). They're in High School, but when they get on the bus with him, they try and push and shove him around too. I still don't like what he's doing to me, but maybe **I** **understand** a bit better why he might be doing it.

Chapter eleven
So what do we do next?

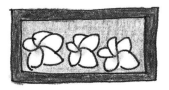

Then (gulp) Teresa said the next thing was for me to go back to school so I could try these new things out. Well, I'll tell you, you know that new **BIG BRAVE** me?? He shrank back down to being the LITTLE OLD PIPSQUEAK me again!!! Could I only be the **BIG BRAVE** me if I was in Teresa's office? Could I be the New Magnificent Me with the real Sam in the real school yard?

So I told Teresa I was worried that when I was actually in front of Sam my brain would turn to mush, my legs would turn to jelly and I wouldn't remember what I was supposed to do.

57

We thought about this together for a while and came up with <u>**five "Sh"**</u> <u>**words**</u> which I could mark off on my fingers (the first of them starts with an "s" not a "sh", but we thought this was okay if it helped me remember). This is what they were:

■ <u>**Sh**</u>**tand** up <u>**sh**</u>**traight** (make sure your body is in position)

■ <u>**Sh**</u>**rug** ("Whatever", "Who cares?")

■ <u>**Sh**</u>**ield** (switch on your personal force shield)

■ <u>**Sh**</u>**are** (a new

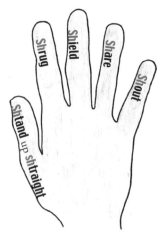

ball, new friends)

■ **Sh**out (if you need help, let others know)

Teresa said everybody worries about not being able to be the new person; so I needed to keep practising with my family. She said Mum and Dad and even Harriet would have to help me practise. They would be the bullies, and I would practise being the new, big, brave me. I thought it might be a good idea to take the week off school to practise a bit more, but Teresa said it was **really important** to keep going back to school every day so I could try our new tips out. **Eeekkk!!**

Chapter twelve
Face off time

So, the next day I went back to school. Boy oh boy, was **I SCARED!** I thought about asking Mum and Dad if I  could go to the dentist to have a few teeth out, or maybe to the doctor to have my legs chopped off instead, but they said I would be **fine** — I

just needed to **remember** what
Teresa had taught me.

The bullying started again first thing
in the morning. We were all working
on the floor when Sam jumped up
to get something from the other
side of the classroom. As he got up,
he carefully STOMPED across
my work. He looked down to make

sure the paper was scrunched and said "So, how did you like that Bonehead?"

I looked up at him, thought about my *Personal Force Shield* (and felt it lock into place) and said "Whatever." Then I turned around, smoothed out my paper and got back to talking to my group.

Sam didn't move, so I looked up again. He had this **REALLY SURPRISED** look on his face. I began to feel **a bit braver** (but still scared too), so I said "What's wrong Bonehead? Did you forget what you got up for?"

Then Sam looked really angry
(which made me feel pretty horrible
inside). But he just said "No **loser**,
only YOU forget stuff!"

And then **something
amazing** happened. Something
that had never happened before —
Sam walked away!! (Yes, that's right,
you heard correctly — *Sam walked
away!).* Usually, he would have done
something more, like stomp on my
book again, or something else nasty.
But he just walked away — because
I had answered him and acted like
I didn't care! I felt like a million

fireworks had gone off inside me! It had actually worked! **Yay me!!**

Chapter thirteen
The really scary time

Well, remember how I was worried before school? You should have seen how SCARED I was before break time! Even though the tough new me had worked on Sam once, I knew that in the classroom our teacher could stop Sam from beating me to a pulp, but in the playground, all kinds of bad things could happen. My heart started **thump!ng** so loudly I thought everyone would be able to hear it and my legs started feeling like they were made of jelly.

But then I thought about how Sam had walked away and how amazing I had felt. So maybe, just maybe, I could use some more of **Teresa's Terrific Tips**. As we left the classroom, I leant down and touched my toes to activate my  again. This time I felt the **ZING** as it locked into place and brought

some confidence with it. I suddenly remembered the new handball in my school bag, and decided to try one more tip — I would find a new group of friends.

So, as I left the classroom, I called out to a kid I know from soccer and said, "Joe, do you want to play handball? My dad got me a new one yesterday!" Joe gave me a big grin, and grabbed his friends Frankie, Tom, JJ and Nick to play too. When we started playing, Christopher and George came and joined in as well. And before you knew it, **we were all** playing **together** — and it was my ball!! I felt so proud and so pleased this was working, just like

Teresa had said it might.

But then the **BAD STUFF STARTED.** Sam came over. He grabbed my new ball and said, "So what's this Loser, a new toy?" I tried to grab it, but he just kept waving it from one side of my face to the other, daring me to grab it.

But then I remembered what Teresa had said about **standing my ground** and not arguing. So, I stood still and calmly said, "Give it back Sam. Stop being a pain."

Sam looked **REALLY** surprised. I

had never spoken to him like that.
Usually, I would have kept trying to
jump for the ball and I would never
have told him to stop doing anything.
But then he did something really bad,

he threw the ball up onto the roof. It bounced a bit and then dribbled down to land in the gutter.

Well, that made me so **MAD**, I did something I never would have done before. I **pretended** I wasn't angry, smirked and said, "Is that as far as you can throw? And I thought you were so strong!"

Well, Sam's face turned the **colour of beetroot**, and you could see he was about to say or do something even worse. But then the **next amazing** thing happened. Christopher came and stood next to me. He didn't say anything. He didn't need to. He just **stood next to me** and looked at Sam.

Well, Sam looked at me, and Christopher and I looked at Sam. And then Sam walked away — **AGAIN!** Okay, he was muttering "**losers**..." but he didn't seem quite so strong and tall anymore. In fact, he looked a lot like a balloon that had just had all the air let out of it.

And **THEN**, just as he walked away, this bird flew past and did something so funny we all nearly died laughing. It did a **huge poo** on Sam's shoulder!! Sam stopped dead in his tracks, looked at his shoulder, saw

the poo trickling down his shirt
and a look of HORROR spread all over
his face. Then, he *RAN* to the boys'
bathroom. Joe and all my new

friends broke up laughing. Damien and the other mean boys didn't seem to know what to do — now their fearless leader had bird poo all over his shirt — so they SLUNK OFF after him.

Christopher turned around and grinned, "Why don't we get a teacher to get that ball down, so I can have a turn."

Chapter fourteen
Bird poo saves the day

Well, I have to say, after that Sam never had quite the same power over me again. The next time I saw Teresa, I told her about the bird poo and she laughed so hard she almost cried. She reminded me though of all the things I had done **before** the bird poohed on Sam. I had activated my *Personal Force Shield*, I had showed I didn't care by saying *"Whatever"* and I had taken **a new thing** to do (the handball) and tried it out with a new bunch of people. She said that these things had helped even more than the bird poo — but she still loved the fact that Sam had been poohed on.

Teresa asked what had happened since then. I said the best thing was I now didn't have to imagine Sam with big fake rubber ears on whenever I see him to make me feel **less frightened**, I just imagine him with a big blob of bird poo in his hair. Works every time!!

Since then, things have really changed for me at school. I now have a **new group of friends** and we just don't bother about Sam and his friends anymore. I have learnt how to be a good friend too, and if Sam or the other boys try to bully anyone else, I go and stand next to

them, to show them that they are not alone. I remember how much it helped me when Christopher showed me some support, so I try and do it for others too.

So now school is actually pretty cool. I've good friends and Sam doesn't seem so mean, because he really doesn't have anyone he can pick on anymore. When we choose teams for sport, someone always seems to **choose me**. I have kids over for a play at my house or else I go to their places. I saw Teresa for five or six more sessions and **practised the tips**. I've stopped seeing her now, but it's good to know that if there is another problem, I can always go and see her again. And every time I see a bird in the playground at school? I have to say, **I give it a little bit of my lunch.**

Parent/Teacher Guides

Information about Bullying

While we all know that every child has the right to feel safe at home, at school and in the community, research indicates that on average, **one in five children** is being bullied at school at any given time. While many parents recall being bullied themselves, bullying **should not be seen as a normal part of growing up**. Research indicates that bullying behaviour doesn't usually go away on its own and often gets worse with time. Thus, it needs to be dealt with directly. In order for it to stop, adults need to support children who seek their help. They should **respond immediately** and take **preventative steps** in order to stop the bullying behaviour from continuing.

The first step is **recognising** when a bullying problem has occurred. This can be extremely difficult, as children **often feel embarrassed** or **afraid of the ramifications** of reporting bullying behaviour. Parents can also feel embarrassed about the perceived lack of relationship between them and their child when the length of time and the extent of the bullying behaviour comes to light. Rest assured however that **children very rarely immediately tell their parents they are being bullied**. A delay is **usual rather than unusual** and is not a reflection of a poor relationship or a lack of trust between you and your child.

• What is bullying?

Bullying is defined as an **abuse of power** (either real or perceived), by someone who is more powerful directed at someone who is having difficulty in standing up to their behaviour. In groups of friends, this power imbalance can be as simple as one child feeling that their other friends will not support them against the bully when the behaviour occurs. As a result, they can often feel isolated and unsupported.

Bullying behaviour is defined as any of the behaviours below:

- physical aggression (pushing, shoving, kicking, hitting)
- verbal aggression (threats, name calling, teasing, swearing)
- passive-aggression (exclusion, malicious gossiping, spreading rumours, ignoring, isolation from the group, stares, whispers)
- cyber bullying (email, social internet sites, text messaging)

To be labelled as bullying, these behaviours usually **occur over a period of time**, rather than being a one off incident. In this book, **overt** (or direct) bullying is defined as consisting of physical and verbal aggression and **covert** (indirect) bullying is defined as passive aggression and cyber bullying.

In schools, there are generally **specific ages** at which bullying is most prevalent. These are: Year 2 (aged 7–8 years), Year 5 (aged 10–11 years) and Year 8 (aged 14–15 years). Whilst bullying occurs in every age group, these ages tend to be when it is reported the most.

81

• The bullying dynamic

The bullying dynamic is generally seen as consisting of the bully, the bully's henchmen, bystanders and the victim. It looks like this:

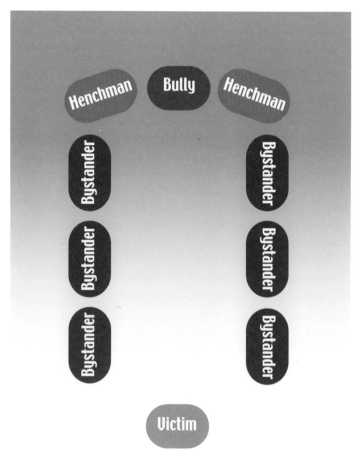

The roles can be defined as follows:

The Bully: the instigator of the bullying. This is the person who usually thinks about how and when the bullying is to be done and enlists the henchmen to help out (this is the same for both boys and girls).

The Henchmen: assist the bully in carrying out the bullying. Interestingly however, if the bully is absent, the henchmen will not usually carry on the bullying alone and may even be friends with the victim. This makes it even more confusing for the victim, as these "fair weather friends" will be friendly one day and tormentors another.

The Bystanders: these are other children that observe/witness the bullying but do nothing about it. In an ideal situation it is these children we need to empower to stand up to the bullies and confront them about their behaviour or to befriend the victim. In this book, Christopher takes on the role of moving from bystander to friend.

The Victim: the person who is the target of the bullying.

• Difference between bullying and normal conflicts/teasing

It is however important to discriminate between children's **normal conflicts**, where two children of an equal power base fall out for a small period, compared to bullying, where the negative actions are repeated in a **purposeful way** over a **period of time**. Either the **intensity** or the **length of time** the behaviours have been occurring confirms the bully's perceived power over the victim. In bullying, **behaviours are targetted towards the intended child in a purposeful way** — with the **intent to cause harm or distress** and to **further establish dominance** over the victim.

83

In most cases, bullying depends on **where** someone is, **not who they are**. For example, a child may be a bully at school, but a victim of excessive authoritarianism and/or punishment at home.

• Short and Long term effects of bullying

Bullying can have short term effects (such as bruising or injury etc). However the worst damage is to a child's sense of self and emotional well-being.

Other research has shown that the effects of bullying **can last more than 25 years**. Many adults can give you specific examples of how they were bullied at school and many school reunions serve as an informal place for people to apologise and repair damage they caused at school.

• Every school has to have an anti-bullying policy

It is now **mandatory** for every school in Australia and many other countries to have a **School Anti-Bullying Policy**. For some schools, this is reinforced by their ethical framework. Other schools have an anti-bullying policy, but **do not have systems in place** to actually work actively with the children when bullying occurs. If bullying is happening at your school, then enquire as to what the action plan is going to be to address it. It is no good having a policy if there is no action to go with it! If you are a parent you are completely **within your rights** to insist on seeing the policy and then defining with the Principal the Action Plan that is going to take place to ensure your child's safety and emotional well-being.

84

Parent Guide

• What you can do to help

Often children do not let their parents know there is a problem. Once the parents find out however, they usually have a very strong protective reaction. This can range from wanting to thump the bully (dads often feel like this) to wanting to confront the bully's parents, to wanting to confront and "warn off" the individual child, to wanting to let everyone else in the school community know what is happening. A word of advice — despite all of these feelings being valid; do not act upon them!!

The best way to confront bullying in schools is to **let the school handle it** — under your watchful eye. Some schools will leap into action and things will change for your child immediately. Other schools may not know what to do with the information and imply that your child is the problem. Every school should have a "whole school" bullying approach, rather than treating bullying as a one off incident between two children. If they don't, then you should help instigate their recognition of the need for a "whole school" bullying approach. On average however, a start up "whole school" bullying approach will take about **18 months** to introduce and implement; so if your child is being bullied, you should not wait for it to come into effect! Talk to the school about what you can all do in the meantime.

• Who you should talk to for help

In the first instance, **use the school resources**. Talk to the Principal, your child's teacher and the Counsellor. Depending upon the problem you could then ask for further

85

assistance from a Clinical Psychologist or Psychologist who is experienced in working with children.

• What to do if your child is being bullied

Help your child learn skills which will reduce the likelihood of bullying:

- teach your child the Tough Talking Game at home;
- help them to be flexible in their thinking and to develop a "Plan B" approach if their "Plan A" isn't working out;
- help them to build a support network.

• What to do if your child is the bully

Children who bully need to replace their aggressive (kicking, punching, pointing, swearing) or passive–aggressive behaviours (whispers, stares, malicious gossip, exclusion etc) with assertive, empathic behaviours. This will usually mean that you need to change your parenting style to help demonstrate to your child what these behaviours look like.

Children who bully often need:

- **warmth and involvement** from their parents;
- **strong boundaries and consistent messages** about acceptable and unacceptable behaviours;
- clear statements that you **do not approve of**, and **will not tolerate**, any bullying behaviour;
- **good times** with parents playing games etc;
- **good supervision** by parents to monitor their activities;
- **clear and consistent rules** within the family as to what is acceptable behaviour;
- **praise and rewards** for when they keep to the behavioural limits;

86

• **firm but non-physical discipline** — removal of privileges or treats when they transgress acceptable behavioural limits.

• **modelling** of appropriate **pro-social behaviours** within your own friendship group.

• **building up of their self-esteem** with things they can do well.

• **inclusion in pro-social activities** such as group sports etc.

There are many websites on the short and long term psychological and lifestyle impacts on children who have been bullied and those who are bullies. This book can't cover everything — **so check them out!**

Teacher Guide

Teachers in classrooms with children who are either bullies or being bullied can often feel unsupported and helpless. As stated above, research has shown that the **best outcomes** for children in schools is where there is a **"whole school"** approach to bullying and where there is a strong message from the Principal down that **bullying is not accepted**. Again, there are many websites which give examples of the "whole school" approach to bullying, which is beyond the scope of this book. I have however provided some questions you can ask while reading this book with the class and some group exercises you could try out.

Class Exercises

These are exercises you can do with your class, either chapter by chapter or else select out the ones you feel are most appropriate. I would recommend the exercises for **Chapters Eight, Nine and Thirteen** as being the most useful for all classes to do, as they break the Tough Talking Game into bite-sized chunks and help the children practise the techniques.

Chapter One

Suggested questions/exercises:

▶ Why do you think Ben might be trying to pretend the bullying is happening to "his friend" and not him? (shame, embarrassment, trying to get ideas from his parents without owning the problem).

❱ Why do you think Ben might not be wanting to tell his parents about the bullying? (embarrassment, not sure about their response)

❱ Which words describe the bullying behaviour? (pushing, shoving, kicking, name calling, hiding his lunch)

> **Group Exercise: Talk about what it might feel like to have a secret which you are not sure if you can tell your parents (hard to keep a secret from your parents, scared they will find out, worried they might be cross with you and not the problem).**

❱ Why do you think Ben's parents might not have given Ben any advice or listened to him seriously from the beginning? (they didn't realise it was important, they didn't realise it was about him).

Chapter Two

Suggested questions/exercises:

❱ Why do you think Ben might not have wanted to tell his parents, even when they had worked out what the problem was? (embarrassment at what had been happening, hard to say he was being bullied, worried his parents might not understand, not sure they can actually help with the problem, worried they might actually make the problem worse).

❱ What do you think of Harriet's response to the problem?

Chapter Three

Suggested questions/exercises:

▶ What do you think of how Mum dealt with Harriet? (appropriate, she should have got into trouble)

▶ How do your parents talk to you if you have a problem?

▶ What do you think about Ben's mum telling the Principal?

▶ Do you think it will make the bullying worse? Why or why not?

Chapter Four

Suggested questions/exercises:

▶ Why do you think Ben might have had a sore tummy?

▶ Why didn't Mum let Ben stay in bed?

▶ What do you do when you are worried about something?

▶ Is there a place in your body that feels different when you are worried? (sore tummy, headaches, butterflies in tummy, nightmares, needing to go to the bathroom)

Chapter Five

Suggested questions/exercises:

▶ What did Ben do at playtime at school?

▶ What do you think Sam and Damien were talking about with Mr Johnson?

▶ What do you think Mr Johnson said to them?

▶ How do you think Sam and Damien are feeling?

❱ Do you think that things will change now the bullies have met with the Principal? (listen to this answer carefully, as it will tell you the childrens' perception of how bullying is managed at your school)

Chapter Six

Suggested questions/exercises:

❱ What does Ben learn when he goes to see Teresa?

❱ What is overt bullying?

❱ Have you ever seen any overt bullying?

❱ What is covert bullying?

❱ Have you ever seen any covert bullying?

Chapter Seven

Suggested questions/exercises:

❱ What examples did Ben give Teresa of how he had been bullied? (physical abuse, verbal abuse, exclusion)

❱ What had Ben already tried to do to stop the bullying?

❱ What did Teresa notice about the way Ben was sitting?

❱ Why did Ben begin to feel excited?

Chapter Eight

Suggested questions/exercises:

❱ What was on Teresa's Action Plan?

❱ What did Teresa mean by "expose the bully?"

❱ What was the Tough Talking Game?

Group Exercise:

1. Get a child out the front of the class (don't pick the weakest in the class or the traditional victim, but rather one of the weaker children who could still benefit).

2. Get them to model the voice and stance of the Tough Talking Game.

3. Have the other children make constructive suggestions as to what else they could do to look strong and confident.

4. Give lots of praise to the child for their new modelling of strong and confident behaviour.

Group Exercise:

1. Choose two different children.

2. Ask the class for the typical nasty things children will say in the playground.

3. Get one of the children to be the bully and to repeat these.

4. Ask the other child (the pretend victim) to answer with "Whatever", "I don't care" type statements, while looking at pretend rubber earlobes on the bully.

5. Ask the "victim" to talk about what they were feeling when they pretended to not care about what the bully was saying.

What was the Personal Force Shield?

How do you switch it on?

Do you think it is a good idea to walk away when someone is being mean?

Why did Teresa suggest that she and Ben needed to make a map of the playground?

Are there any places in our school where bullying is more likely to occur?

Group Exercise:

1. Make a map of the school and mark out where bullying is more likely to happen.

2. Identify where the playground duty teacher usually stands.

3. Talk with the children about where the safest parts of the playground are and the best places to play.

Why would meeting new people make a difference for Ben?

Group Exercise:

1. How do you ask other kids if you can join in their game? (elicit answers from the group and then role play them with children out the front of the class)

Chapter Nine

Suggested questions/exercises:

> **Group Exercise:**
>
> 1. Get children to pair up. Tell one half of the pair they are to be the bully and they are to say something nasty (provide possible statements, such as "You're a loser, you can't play with us"). Get the other half of the pair to pretend to be a victim of bullying and to cry. Check out how each of the pair were feeling (bully should feel powerful and strong, victim should feel small and weak).
>
> 2. Get them to swap roles so that both have the same experience (and so there is no residual power imbalance between them — remember not to get children to pair up who may be a real life bully/victim pair.
>
> 3. Now get them to do it again. The bully says the same nasty things again, but the victim is to assume the posture and voice of the Tough Talking Game. Get them to lock in their Personal Force Shield and say "whatever" and walk away and then to pretend to ask another person to play.
>
> 4. Get both children to be the bully and the victim.
>
> 5. Get the children to reflect on the difference between when they were powerless and when they could follow the Tough Talking Game recommendations.

Chapter Ten

Suggested questions/exercises:

▶ What are some of the reasons why bullies might be bullies?

▶ Do you think children are sometimes mean or angry when they are actually feeling sad underneath?

Chapter Eleven

Suggested questions/exercises:

▶ What did Ben and Teresa decide was the best way to remember the tips?

Group Exercise:

Hold up your hand and ask the children to label the 5 "sh" things that Ben could use to remember Teresa's Terrific Tips.

Why did Ben not want to go back to school the next day?

Chapter Twelve

Suggested questions/exercises:

▶ Why did Ben want to go to the dentist or have his legs chopped off?

▶ What was the first thing Sam said or did to Ben the next day?

▶ What did Ben do?

❯ What happened?

How did Ben feel?

> **Group Exercise:**
>
> 1. Get the children to pair up.
>
> 2. Ask one of them to be Ben and one of them to be Sam.
>
> 3. Role play out the scene from the book.
>
> 4. Ask all the "Ben's" how they felt to go from being scared, to trying something different.
>
> 5. Then ask all the "Sam's" about what they had been expecting when they trod on Ben's work compared to what they felt when he answered them back.

Chapter Thirteen

Suggested questions/exercises:

❯ Why was Ben even more scared before break time?

❯ What could Ben do now?

> **Group Exercise:**
>
> ❯ Hold up your hand and reinforce the 5 "sh" reminders as to what Ben could do now (stand up straight, shrug, shield, share, shout)
>
> ❯ Which ones of these did Ben choose?
>
> ❯ What did Sam do next?

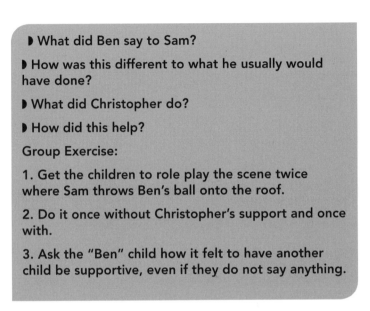

▶ What did Ben say to Sam?

▶ How was this different to what he usually would have done?

▶ What did Christopher do?

▶ How did this help?

Group Exercise:

1. Get the children to role play the scene twice where Sam throws Ben's ball onto the roof.

2. Do it once without Christopher's support and once with.

3. Ask the "Ben" child how it felt to have another child be supportive, even if they do not say anything.

Chapter Fourteen

Suggested questions/exercises:

▶ What did Teresa say that Ben had done well?

▶ How has life changed for Ben now?

▶ What does he do now that was different from what he was doing before?

▶ Why did he keep seeing Teresa for a while? (importance of practising the tips)

▶ Why does he give the birds a little bit of his lunch?

Finishing the book

Suggested questions/exercises:

▶ What did you like about this book?

▶ What did you learn?

> **Group Exercise:**
>
> Prepare a box with a slit in the top. Give all students two pieces of paper with an a) and b) listed on both. Ask them to identify:
>
> 1. On the first piece of paper, a) who they see as being bullied in their class and b) who is doing the bullying.
>
> 2. On the second piece of paper — How they would like bullying to be dealt with at your school. a) what should the rules be? and b) what should the consequences be?

Acknowledgments

A book doesn't come together without a huge amount of thought and input from many others. I know that I have probably not mentioned many of those who have contributed with time, thoughts and wisdom — and for that I apologise; however I would like to say a HUGE thank you to the following:

Pen, Caroline and Ann — my Sunday night movie, dinner, proofreading and constructive critic girls. Thank you for your unending patience, love and feedback — absolutely invaluable.

Julia and Chris — for your continual support and extremely useful feedback — all of which has been incorporated!

The staff of Lindfield Children's Bookshop — for their encouragement and constructive reading
Mum/Grandma and James
Justine Blunt
The Fahmy Family — Caroline, Emil, Christopher and George
The Sommers-Blunt family — George, Laura and Ruby
Claudia
The Reid family — Michael, Joe and Frank
Prue Reid
The Jaensch family — Anna, Tony, Tom, Jaime and Nick
Inger Osborn
The Ruinet family — Kristel, Mark, Annabelle and Harry
The Stewart family — Lise-Lotte, Richard, Anne-Lise and William
The Lee family — Jacks, Steve, Finn, Sophie and James
The Fraser family — Carrie, David, James, Tori and Ally
The Blunt family — Tony, Ange, Emily, Tomos, William and Michael
The Metcalf family — Pen, Graham, Antonia and Cara. A special thank you to Pen for her bird poo solutions!
The Rigby family — Caroline, Simon, Annabel, Nick, Millie and Charlie
The Rapee family — Wendy, Ron, Alice and Lucy

The Philipson family — Jo, Lindsay, Sarah and Kate
The Dalland family — Julia, James, Alex and Emily
The Rateb family — Elaine, Zohdy, Ayesha and Ahlia
The Elliott family — Greg, Marie, Rebecca, Madeline and Jacob
The children of Lynton Downs School, Kaikoura; who were so hospitable and allowed Chloe and me to use them to test drive our "work in progress."
Nickola Blunt — for all of her love and creativity.
Virginia
Theresa, Tony and Sarah
Ellie and Kevin Bailey
Nick Rigby — for specifically ringing me up to share his thoughts on the book
Antonia Metcalf — for her very useful thoughts on name spelling
The children, families and staff of Killara Public School and Ravenswood — who support our family through love, friendship and in so many other ways...

With love,
Lucy and Chloe

Beating *the* bullies ——————————————————